The
Future
of Farting

by
Dr Barry Guff

The Future of Farting

---

by
Dr Barry Guff

Michael O'Mara Books Limited

First published in Great Britain in 2013 by
Michael O'Mara Books Limited
9 Lion Yard
Tremadoc Road
London SW4 7NQ

A CIP catalogue record for this book is available from the British Library.

Papers used by Michael O'Mara Books Limited are natural, recyclable products made from wood grown in sustainable forests. The manufacturing processes conform to the environmental regulations of the country of origin.

ISBN: 978-1-78243-177-0 in paperback print format

1 3 5 7 9 10 8 6 4 2

www.mombooks.com

Cover design by Greg Stevenson; designed and typeset by Greg Stevenson
Printed and bound in China

Contents

Introduction

After *The History of Farting* made ripples in the
literary world, my publisher kindly sent me ten
dozen tins of baked beans to ensure that I could
produce a follow-up. It has therefore been my
joy and a profound relief to pen a tome about
this most misunderstood of bodily functions.

My interest in farting stemmed from my late
grandfather who, during frequent bouts of passing
gas, uttered many wise words on the subject –
although the stench was so bad that I never
ventured near enough to hear them. One of the
great joys of breaking wind is that element of
surprise. Although nerve endings in the sphincter
let you know that a fart is waiting to be released,

when you actually let it rip you're never quite sure what you're going to get. Will it stink, will it be noisy? I can only compare the anticipation to pulling a Christmas cracker.

However, we should never underestimate the power of a fart. The fart is our master. It rarely arrives to order, often choosing to go public at the moment when it can cause us maximum embarrassment. And how many times have we smugly congratulated ourselves on successfully suppressing one, only to be caught out moments later by its evil twin? Of course, I appreciate that not everyone makes a song and dance about farting, which is a shame because *Arseblast: the Musical* is one I would pay to see.

So what does the future hold? Flatulence technology is by no means stagnant. There are suggestions for a sealable fart bag that you wear inside your underpants and which collects your toots for your later enjoyment.

Meanwhile, police officers are being encouraged to adopt high-fibre diets and to store their farts in containers as a cheap alternative to CS gas. After centuries of bad press, it is high time that personal gas was used in a positive manner. Remember: the future's bright, the future's brownish. Happy farting!

Dr Barry Guff, 2013

The Science of Farts

Why do we fart?

When we swallow too much air or eat foods with
which the human digestive system cannot easily
cope, excess gas becomes trapped in our stomach
or intestines. The only way for this excess gas to exit
the body is through the anus in the form of flatulence.
If we never farted, the gas would be reabsorbed into
the blood and poison us, so basically farting is
nature's way of releasing our own toxins.
Farting is therefore a good thing.

What's in a fart?

The principal gases found in a fart are nitrogen, oxygen, carbon dioxide, hydrogen and methane. Of these methane is the killer. Otherwise known as marsh gas, it is produced by the decomposition of organic matter and is highly flammable, thus encouraging the foolhardy, inspired by the Doors' classic '(C'mon Baby) Light My Fart' to attempt to set fire to their guffs, a stunt that usually ends in a round of applause and a trip to the hospital to get a new bottom.

Nevertheless by themselves these gases won't create the distinctive aroma that we have come to know and love. That comes from a heady mix of methylindole (produced when methane combines with indole, an organic compound created by decomposing proteins), skatole (a gas formed from carbon, hydrogen and nitrogen, which ominously take its name from *skatos*, the Greek word for dung) and last, but by no means least, hydrogen sulphide, the infamous rotten-egg gas. Although the stench may be overwhelming, the average fart contains less than 0.5 per cent hydrogen sulphide,

which is some indication of its potency. As well
as possessing a foul stink, hydrogen sulphide is
extremely poisonous, corrosive, flammable and
explosive, so it's no wonder some of your chuffs turn
out the way they do. Interestingly methylindole and
skatole are also used in making perfume. Hydrogen
sulphide definitely isn't, unless you have an
unusual taste in perfumes.

What colour is a lit fart?

Fart lighting or pyroflatulence is the practice of igniting the gases produced by human flatulence, often producing a flame of a blue hue, hence the act being known colloquially as a 'blue angel' or 'blue dart'. Other colours of flame such as orange and yellow are possible depending on the mixture of gases formed in the colon.

FART FACT #1

Continuous farting for six
years and nine months would
create energy equal to that
of an atomic bomb.

Are ordinary farts invisible?
Usually, although on a cold day they may produce a small cloud of steam, like breath from your mouth. Hopefully that is where the similarity ends. If not, try chewing some mints.

What causes a fart to be noisy?
That lovely trumping sound is the result of vibration when internal pressure forces the gas out through your sphincter. The level of noise varies according to the velocity of the fart and the tightness of the ringpiece muscles.

Why do silent farts smell worse than noisy ones?

Huge ripping farts are usually the result of carbohydrates fermenting in your intestines to produce large amounts of carbon dioxide, which is an odourless gas. Consequently such farts are loud but relatively innocuous. By contrast tiny farts are mostly caused by anaerobic fermentation, which produces a lot of methane and sulphides. The sulphides in particular stink. It is possible, however, to make a lot of carbon dioxide and sulphides at the same time to create a stinky ripper. People who are able to accomplish this feat on a regular basis earn widespread admiration from fellow farteurs and a lifetime ban from McDonald's.

Why do farts linger around at nostril level?
Carbon dioxide – found in high levels in farts – is heavier than air, and therefore keeps farts at a low level rather than allowing the lighter gases, like nitrogen, to waft them up to the ceiling where they could be enjoyed only by flies and moths.

FART FACT #2

It is considered good for your health
to fart between fifteen and twenty-five
times a day (based on an average fart
time length of 1.2 seconds). The scientific
recommendation is 18 to 30 seconds of
farts per day. Since on average we only
fart fourteen times a day, the message is
clear: we are simply not farting enough.
Time to hit the beer and beans.

Why do beans make us fart so much?

Beans contain sugars that humans can't digest.
When these sugars reach our intestines, the bacteria
in our body go crazy, enjoy a big feast and make
industrial amounts of gas.

Why do hot farts smell so bad?

Heat is a by-product of the bacterial fermentation
and digestion processes that create pungent gas.
Temperature is a critical ingredient in determining
how your trump will emerge – the hotter the fart,
the faster it spreads. This is because air particles

have more energy at higher temperatures, so there is more diffusion of the gas. That's why curries and hot spices are so sought-after by connoisseurs of flatulence.

Are farts acid, neutral or alkaline?

Farts tend to be rich in carbon dioxide, and, as we have seen, may also contain hydrogen sulphide. If a fart were to be dissolved in water, carbon dioxide would react with water to produce carbonic acid, and hydrogen sulphide would make hydrosulphuric acid. These are both weak acids, so farts (at least when in solution) are mildly acidic.

Is it possible to freeze farts, and would they still be smelly after they are defrosted?

The water vapour components of farts would freeze quite readily, but to freeze the entire fart would require high pressure and low temperature conditions such as those used to produce dry ice. The fart's composition would be unchanged by the process, and hence would still be smelly upon reversion to the gaseous state, but the conditions required probably rule out trying this in the home.

Is it true that talking too much can make you fart?

Yes. People who swallow a lot of air fart more than those who don't. Much of this air is swallowed while we eat, so people who talk while eating or who chew with their mouth open will take in more air. A considerable quantity of the air is released immediately in the form of a belch but the rest travels down through the small intestine where it forms intestinal gas – or a fart, to put it in layman's terms.

Why do farts always smell worse in the bath?
This is because the fart molecules percolate through the water and form chemical bonds with the water molecules before emerging into the air. These water-based fart molecules are heavier than the normal air-based fart molecules and therefore tend to linger longer at low levels instead of dispersing. Also, the scent sensation is intensified in the bath because you are sitting directly above the source of the smell.

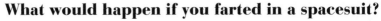

What would happen if you farted in a spacesuit?
Quite simply, it would be the worst fart ever because there
would be nowhere for it to escape and therefore the smell
would stay with you all the way back to the space station.

**So why couldn't you open a butt-flap in
your suit to let the gas out?**
Because if you did, your blood would boil. The
temperature of your blood is normally around 37°C and
is kept liquid by the pressure of the Earth's atmosphere.
But in space there is no atmosphere, so at 37°C your

blood would boil and expand. A spacesuit prevents this happening by keeping the body under constant pressure but if you were to release this pressure – by opening a butt-flap to release a fart – the suit would cease to work. As your blood boiled and expanded, this would cause your skin and organs to swell up. And that's not even the worst of it. If you found yourself in a shaded area – say with Earth between you and the Sun – the temperature in space would drop to well below –100°C. Your spacesuit is insulated to stop you losing heat but if you were to open a flap, the heat would fly out and you would freeze solid in a matter of seconds. So all things considered, if you fart in space it really is best just to grin and bear it.

FART FACT #3

Theoretically, a fart in space should propel you forward since there is no opposing force in the form of gravity to counteract the force of the fart. However in practice as you have to wear a spacesuit to survive, this would contain the anal blast and virtually suppress any forward propulsion.

Popular Types of Fart

There are almost as many different types of fart as there are species of insect. Sadly, over the centuries, some have become extinct as a result of changing diet and lifestyle, including the once widespread Woolly Mammoth Fart, the involuntary spasm released by Neanderthal Man on realizing that his straw house was about to be trampled underfoot by a woolly mammoth. Meanwhile, at least a dozen other farts remain on the endangered list, and it is our duty

to prevent them from vanishing altogether.
Unfortunately space prevents the inclusion of
the complete list of current farts (i.e. those with
five or more recorded instances in the year
ending 31 December 2013), but here are some
of the most popular:

THE BACK SEAT FART

Long family car journeys are a breeding ground for
flatulence. Sooner or later one of the kids on the
back seat will let one go and, unable to escape, its
odour will eventually fill the entire car until you are

left gasping for air. Your wife will automatically blame you (which is perhaps understandable given that she has shared a bed with you for fifteen years) but although it may be impossible to determine from which direction the stench originated, the stifled giggles will quickly tell you which of the children was responsible.

THE BALLOON FART

In the same way you blow up a balloon and then pull the neck out so that the air escapes with a long squeal, some people can do that with their butt.

The Bullet

A single, loud fart like a gunshot. It may startle
onlookers and the farter alike, but is otherwise
harmless, generally being odour-free.

The Concealed Fart

You're sitting in an important meeting and, to
your horror, you can feel one building up. You
dare not simply let it rip in case it proves audible
to the entire room and several floors below but
at the same time you know it's too far gone to be
held in. So you slowly relax your butt-hole muscles

and let it out oh so gently. It makes no sound and no smell and the only internal sensation is a pleasant, light bubbling like a dip in a Jacuzzi. The Concealed Fart is an important technique to master in order to avoid wholesale embarrassment.

THE ETERNAL

A fart that seems to go on for ever, taking you through several chord changes. Just when you think you have finally reached the end, it has one final toot up its sleeve. The satisfaction and inner peace you feel at the end of such a fart has to be experienced to be believed. All those hippies wasted millions on mind-expanding drugs in the

sixties when they could have achieved the same
sensation with a really good fart.

THE FUFFER

In the build-up it shows all the promise of
being a loud ripper that could shatter glass, but
disappointingly it emerges as nothing more than
a mild puff that barely even registers with other
people in the room. It's like trading in a Rottweiler
for a French poodle. Still, the great thing with
farting is that you know there'll be another one
along soon – and hopefully the next one will
be more satisfying.

THE HOT AND SPICY

A fiery fart that leaves you with a burning sensation and the inability to sit down for a quarter of an hour.

THE INNOCENT

An unannounced fart that slips out without any fuss – no sound, no smell, no trace of its existence. Indeed it is almost imperceptible even to the farter who is able to carry on talking through the moment of expulsion without skipping a beat.

The Losing Gamble
You were sure it was only going to be a fart, but
you were wrong. An excruciatingly embarrassing
experience, especially on a first – and therefore
inevitably last – date.

The Machine Gun
A fart that heralds its arrival with a rapid burst
of gunfire reminiscent of Al Capone.

The OAP Fart

As people get older they often have less control over their bodily functions, which is why the most popular design of tie for a senior gentleman is one with a soup stain already on it. Similarly when old people sneeze or cough, they sometimes fart simultaneously. It saves time and energy. It's like consolidating all your debts into one monthly payment.

The Organic

This is passed by health food fanatics who are so proud of the purity of their fart that they will even ask you to sniff it and compare it to your own putrid offerings. If you can't smell anything, they claim it is proof that their wholesome lifestyle produces a clean, healthy body. Some will even go so far as to fake farts in order to prove their point.

THE ROOM CLEARER
Does exactly what it says on the tin.

THE SBD (SILENT BUT DEADLY)
The most famous fart of all – in fact more a species than a mere type. Like Hitler's V-2 bomb, the SBD offers no warning to innocent bystanders before

releasing its deadly payload – in this case the foul stench
of a month-old rotten egg.

THE TARDY FART

This one seems to hang around inside you for hours.
It stays with you longer than your partner's mother.
You try and force it out at an appropriate moment but
no joy. Then just when you least want – or expect – it,
out it pops with a resounding PARP!

THE TICKLER

A toot so soft and gentle it feels as if your butt is being
caressed with downy feathers.

THE TRUMPET INVOLUNTARY

A long, slow, musical fart that makes it sound as if
you've got Kenny Ball and His Jazzmen up there.
Rich in wind, the Trumpet Involuntary is often the
prelude to a really satisfying crap.

THE TWO-TONE FART

Flatulence in two parts. The first is a high soprano
note, the second a deep bass. Think Maria Callas
and Neil Diamond, but with a different smell.
Unless they'd both been out for a chicken
madras the night before.

Five Steps to Successful Farting

1. Eat the right foods. Try a bowl of prunes and bran
    for breakfast, an apricot for a mid-morning snack,
    followed by a dish of baked beans and lentils for
    lunch, a banana in the afternoon, and then in the
    evening a vegetable curry washed down with a few
    pints of gassy beer. If possible, also try and find time
    for an egg or two because they contain sulphur and
    will therefore give your farts stink appeal. Remember,
    the more vegetables you eat, the more you will fart.
    Broccoli, cabbage, Brussels sprouts, cauliflower,

Jerusalem artichoke, radishes, onions and garlic can all be relied upon to put colour in your cheeks.

2. Unless you're being examined for piles by a doctor or are at that point in the marriage ceremony where the minister says, 'If anyone has any objections to this union, please speak up now,' or you are playing the front end of a pantomime horse, never try to hold a fart in. It's like trying to restrain a tiger with a piece of string. Instead relax, set it free, liberate it, release

it from its anal shackles and ride it as if you were
surfing a wave. Enjoy the short journey, wherever it
may take you.

3. It is a curious fact that while we love the smell of our
    own farts, we are repulsed by the stench of anyone
    else's – and if not repulsed, jealous. Consequently
    sniffing our own farts is one of life's great guilty
    pleasures – along with squeezing pimples and licking
    the lid of an ice cream carton. The best way to
    appreciate your fart is to stick your head between your
    knees as soon as you know one is coming and inhale

deeply. This is a perfectly safe practice – nobody
has ever died from inhaling their own gas.
However, under no circumstances should
you attempt to enhance the experience by
farting while sitting inside a tied plastic bin
bag. The actual fart won't kill you but the lack
of oxygen will.

4. Never deliberately try to release a veritable
cheek flapper when you're hopelessly drunk
because at best you will probably produce fart
art (skid marks) and at worst you will fill your

underpants in a way you haven't managed
since you grew out of Pampers.

5. Never wear white underpants.

FART FACT #4

The 1970s UK pop and glam rock band
Kenny were originally called Chuff. It
was probably a wise decision to change
their name from a synonym for 'fart'
especially as one of their biggest hits
was 'Fancy Pants'.

Farts in the News

Serial Farter

In 2007, a social club in Devon banned a seventy-seven-year-old man from breaking wind while indoors. Retired bus driver Maurice Fox received a letter from Kirkham Street Sports and Social Club in Paignton which said: 'After several complaints regarding your continual breaking of wind while in the club, would you please consider that your actions are considered disgusting to fellow members and visitors. You sit close to the front

door, so would you please go outside when required.'
A club regular for twenty years, Fox said that the letter was a surprise because he had not been given a formal warning. 'I think someone has complained about the noise,' he said. 'I am a loud farter, but there is no smell.'

Little Stinker

Everyone farts, sure. But is it okay to fart in class? Well at the Spectrum Jr/Sr High School in Stuart, Florida, teachers decided to take severe action when a twelve-year-old boy was proving to be a public menace. On 4 November 2008, teacher D.C. Carden reported the child after he 'continually disrupted his classroom environment by breaking wind and shutting off several computers'. The boy was placed under arrest by Warren F. Pettway of the Martin County Sheriff Office and questioned at the scene until he confessed to his cheese cutting. He was then charged with 'Disruption of a School Function' and released to his mother. No doubt beans were soon off the menu in their household.

FART FACT #5

As the Romans considered holding
in farts to be medically harmful,
the Emperor Claudius passed a law
legalizing farting at banquets.

The Wind Section

Ken Lawrence, an oboist with the Kansas City Symphony Orchestra, was suspended in 1994 after one of the horn players complained that he had farted loudly during a rehearsal for *The Nutcracker*, 'creating an overpowering smell'.

Bring in the Sniffer Dogs

In the ultimate scare story Malawi Justice Minister George Chaponda announced that a law introduced in the country in 2011 would make breaking wind in public a criminal offence. The Local Courts Bill read: 'Any person who vitiates the atmosphere in any place so as to make it noxious to the public shall be guilty of a misdemeanour.' Residents in the country's financial capital Blantyre kicked up a stink when they heard the claim. One college student said he could not understand how the law could be enforced. 'We all fart in public,' he said, 'and it will be difficult to tell who has done it. Some do it silently. Our legislators should not waste our time and money on childish issues. This will not work. We will keep on farting.' A couple of weeks later, a red-faced Mr Chaponda had to apologize, saying the new law did not cover farting after all.

Office Trumper

Swede Göran Andervass was awarded $85,000 compensation in 2003 after a tribunal ruled that he was unfairly dismissed for telling off a co-worker for passing gas. The early-morning flatulence prompted an angry response from Andervass who was suspended and then made redundant after the farter complained to management. 'My colleague was absolutely aware of the awful smell,' said Andervass. 'It was pure provocation.' Commenting on the compensation award, the Swedish Work Environment Authority said: 'If a fart is done on purpose when going into somebody's office, it is important that management takes the matter seriously.'

Escaping Gas

It seems the Swedes have problems with flatulence (maybe it's all that pickled herring they eat) because in 2010 a twenty-one-year-old inmate at Malmö prison was hauled before the authorities for repeatedly and deliberately breaking wind in the direction of the guards. Although the prisoner protested that his farts were all noise and no fragrance, he was warned about his future conduct.

Great Balls of Fire

Still in Scandinavia, arguably the most alarming case of flatulence on record was that of a thirty-year-old Danish man who, while having surgery on his buttocks, broke wind and set his genitals on fire. The operation to remove a mole from the man's backside was being carried out at Kjellerups Hospital in 2002. Surgeon Jorn Kristensen was removing the offending mole with an electric knife when the patient suddenly broke wind, lighting a spark and igniting his genitals, which had previously been washed with surgical spirit. When the man woke up, his penis and scrotum were 'burning like hell'. Dr Kristensen said: 'No one considered the possibility that the man would break wind during the operation, let alone that it would catch fire. It was an unfortunate accident.'

FART FACT #6

The average man releases
enough farts each day to
inflate a small balloon.

Potting the Brown

With the players needing maximum powers of concentration, you can normally hear a pin drop at the World Snooker Championship. But the 2013 semi-final between five-time champion Ronnie O'Sullivan and the appropriately named Judd Trump was interrupted when someone in the audience let rip a monster botty burp that reverberated around Sheffield's Crucible Theatre with such force that it sounded as if the perpetrator had stepped on a duck. Trump, who had been about to take his shot, saw the funny side at first but was less impressed when a second guff slipped out seconds later. This time he turned to glare at the crowd where someone appeared to blame the noisy emission on their breakfast with a shout of 'Weetabix!'

Gas Leak

Police officers who were called to a suspected domestic violence incident in Clawson, Michigan in 2013 found when they arrived that it was simply the screams of a woman objecting to the smell of her boyfriend's farts. A neighbour had reported hearing a loud noise followed by a female voice yelling 'Stop! No!', but the woman in question explained that she had screamed because her boyfriend had continued to pass gas despite being told to stop.

Let it Rip

It's the age-old dilemma: you're trapped in a crowded, confined space – such as a plane – and you can feel that first, ominous twitching in your bowels. Do you try and hold it in all the way to your destination, or do you just let it rip and pray that it doesn't turn out either to be so noisy that it echoes through the entire plane or a real stinker that has your fellow passengers diving for the sick bags? Well, a recent report from the *New Zealand Medical Journal* recommends that, regardless of the smell, when it comes to farting on a plane it is definitely a case of better out than in.

The medics state that people often fart more on flights because of changes in the aircraft cabin pressure but warn that holding them in can cause stress, discomfort, pain, bloating, high blood pressure, pyrosis and dyspepsia. This advice even applies to the cockpit. The report's authors say: 'If the pilot restrains a fart, all the drawbacks previously mentioned, including diminished concentration, may affect his abilities to control the airplane.' Anyway, they add, all your best attempts at restraint can be wrecked in an instant by a sudden jolt of turbulence.

Diverting Smell

A 2006 American Airlines flight from Washington to Dallas was forced to divert to Nashville, Tennessee, after passengers smelled smoke on the plane. It turned out to be the result of a woman passenger lighting matches in the bathroom to cover up the smell of her personal gas. American Airlines banned her from flying with them in future.

Something in the Air

Police officers in Leicester sniffed out a cannabis farm in 2013 – after opening their patrol car windows because the officer in the back kept breaking wind. The cop's deadly gas – the result of having recently adopted a high-protein diet – filled the car with noxious fumes, but when his two choking colleagues decided to let in some fresh air they immediately detected a strong smell of cannabis. Having ascertained that the smell was not emanating from their flatulent friend, they followed their noses and traced it to a house further along the street where they uncovered a cannabis factory with a crop worth £12,000 ($18,000).

A police source said: 'Our officers came up trumps.'

A Fart by Another Name

There are many colourful slang expressions for the act of passing wind, including 'blowing the old bum trumpet', 'floating an air biscuit', 'cracking a rat', 'stepping on a duck', 'trouser coughing' and 'sneezing from the turtle's head'. One of the most obscure is 'cutting the cheese'. This phrase stems from the thick layer of wax that some cheeses have on their exterior and which keeps the odour of the cheese contained as it ages. However once someone

cuts into the wheel of cheese, all the aroma is
released in a stink similar to a fart. So when people
smell something foul, they ask: 'Who cut
the cheese?'

FART FACT #7

Dead people fart – and the chances are
that you will, too. As all the muscles in
the body relax in the period immediately
after death, this allows gas to escape.
Sadly it is the one fart you will never
be able to enjoy.

World Farting Records

Highest Fart

Competing at the 1952 Arizona State Pole Vault
Championships, Ethan Bucksnort had just taken off
when he let loose an almighty ripper, the force of
which enabled him to clear the bar by more than 26
feet and land just over the border in New Mexico.
His extraordinary vault of 40.34 feet (12.3 metres)
was nearly three times higher than the existing

world record but was not officially recognized by the
Amateur Athletic Union as it was wind-assisted.

LONGEST FART

While sitting in the front room of his home in Sofia,
Bulgaria, on 2 May 1965, Olev Dropachuv farted non-
stop for 3 minutes 14.2 seconds, badly staining his
underpants, rupturing his bowels and killing his pet
canary. He explained afterwards that he had been holding
it in for five months and two days ever since he had begun
dating a deeply religious girl with a psychotic father.

Longest Fart (Total Duration)

A Hogmanay blast of gas released by fifty-eight-year-old Jock McGuffie of Inverness, Scotland, in 1999 was still being smelt in the bar of the Dunwhumpin Hotel twenty-three hours later. In the entire history of flatulence McGuffie's butt sneeze is recorded as being the first to have spanned two millennia.

Longest Fart (Individual)

A single bullet fart discharged by Sweden's Sven Aasblast at 7.48 p.m. on 9 December 2011 blew out the windows of his Stockholm house and caused

damage to three surrounding properties. Neighbours
thought it was a terrorist attack until they realized
Sven had been eating pickled reindeer again.

SMELLIEST FART

Appearing in 2012 on the popular UK TV challenge
Where the Fart Is, Alice Queef of Buckinghamshire
produced a silent brown genie that recorded a hitherto
unprecedented score of 184 on the studio Guffometer. Its
stench was likened to that of the carcass of a dead horse
which had been left to rot in the desert sun for six months.
Several members of the studio audience were overcome
by the fumes and one woman was still being treated in

hospital for shock eleven months later. Ms Queef
attributed her success to a fondness for raw liver
and egg.

MOST WIDELY RECEIVED FART
During a sermon at St Saviour's Church, Pratt's
Bottom, Kent, on 11 July 1935, an unannounced
zump from Commander Neville Ripsnorter
was appreciated by the front five rows of the
congregation, a total of 110 people. They then sang
the hymn 'O Lord Safeguard My Passage'.

LARGEST GROUP FART
On 14 May 2002, 135 members of the Utah Bean
Appreciation Society joined forces for a simultaneous
group fart, the force of which was felt more than
3 miles away and which added an estimated 0.0001°C
to the Earth's atmospheric temperature.

FART FACT #8

On a 1964 edition of UK
music show *Top of the Pops*,
DJ Alan Freeman inadvertently
introduced Sounds Orchestral's
'Cast Your Fate to the Wind' as
'Cast Your Wind to the Fate'.

The Blame Game

Unless the guilty party holds his or her hands up
immediately, apportioning the blame for a guff in
a crowded room is a challenge worthy of the
deduction powers of Sherlock Holmes. In the absence
of tangible evidence, you can make light of the
situation among yourselves with this quickfire,
back-and-forth rhyming game – further proof, if
it were needed, that farting can be fun:

Whoever smelt it, dealt it.
Whoever observed it, served it.
Whoever detected it, ejected it.
Whoever refuted it, tooted it.
Whoever sniffed it, biffed it.
Whoever deduced it, produced it.
Whoever said the rhyme did the crime.
Whoever made the joke made the ass smoke.
Whoever spoke last set off the blast.
Whoever's poking fun is the smoking gun.
Whoever said the verse just made the air worse.
He who was a smart-ass has a fart-ass.
The next person who speaks is the person who reeks.

Ask the Doctor

HOW CAN I DISGUISE MY FARTS?

The force with which your butt cheeks vibrate in that all-important pre-fart moment usually helps you determine whether or not your emission will be noisy enough to register on the Richter scale. If you suspect you're about to unleash a veritable bazooka, a practical method for concealing the sound is to produce a fake sneeze, a loud exclamation pertaining to some imaginary, unseen event or even burst into a sudden round of applause for no apparent reason. You may, of course, be required to explain these actions but an accusation of irrational behaviour is probably a small price to pay, unless your partner becomes convinced it means you're having an affair, decides to break up with you and trashes your car. Disguising the smell is altogether trickier. If you are particularly prone to letting go stuff that makes people's eyes water at 100 paces, you could try carrying a can of air freshener around with you and hope that you act in time – a technique known as 'spray and pray'.

DO WOMEN FART AS MUCH AS MEN?

Whereas the average man farts fourteen times a day, a woman's output is nearer nine. So women do release a lot of farts – but they're just not as proud of them as men are. In fact, a study shows that when fed comparable amounts of food, women actually produce more pungent farts than men. But you'll never get them to admit it.

WHAT IS A DEATH FART?

The *Urban Dictionary* defines a death fart as an occasion 'when one farts and it smells as if something has died and is in the process of decaying inside your rectum'. Entire streets have been evacuated following a single death fart.

WHERE DO FARTS GO WHEN YOU HOLD THEM IN?
It is one of life's great mysteries that you hold in
a fart for ages because it would be inconvenient
to release it but then when you're finally ready to
let it go, you find that it has vanished altogether.
So what has happened to it? Has it escaped
without you noticing? The answer is no, it has
simply retreated back into the intestine, where it is
stored waiting to be released at a later date. So it's
comforting to know that you haven't lost the fart,
it's just been delayed.

WHY ARE SOME PEOPLE MORE APPRECIATIVE
OF FARTS THAN OTHERS?

My theory is that it depends on their job. For example,
I used to know a wine taster who loved to smell her own
and anyone else's farts. She would dissect the complexities
of the 'bouquet' as if it were a vintage burgundy, noting:
'I'm getting broccoli, a hint of cabbage, eggs, garlic,
and unless I'm very much mistaken subtle undertones
of rare rump steak.'

DO WE FART IN OUR SLEEP?

Absolutely. In fact, as our partners may sadly testify, we
fart a great deal in our sleep, but because we're asleep we

don't notice it. The exception is if we're startled out of our slumbers by a sudden ripper, but usually we tend to save those for the moment we wake up in the morning.

CAN EXCESSIVE FARTING CAUSE SEXUAL PROBLEMS?
Only if your partner refuses to have sex with you because you're stinking out the place.

WHY DO VEGETARIANS FART MORE?
Because they eat more foods that are high in fibre. However their farts tend to smell less than those of meat eaters and they're also much quieter due

to their larger stools and looser sphincters, both results of their diet. Carnivores have much tighter sphincters, allowing them to blow a mightier horn when farting.

SHOULD I LIGHT MY OWN FARTS?

For medical reasons, the answer has to be no as it is a potentially dangerous practice. However we know that despite years of government health warnings there are still plenty of people who see it as their right to be able to light up. Since 2007 in the UK, lighting farts in enclosed public spaces – such as pubs and restaurants – has been illegal, so customers have to step outside into specially designated areas if they feel the urge to set their anal gases ablaze. Some do this up to forty times a day and buy expensive gold lighters specifically for the purpose. Of course what you do in the privacy of your own home is your prerogative, but always consider the feelings of others who may be present. For example with a casual acquaintance it would be courteous to enquire before removing your underpants: 'Do you mind if I light up?'

AT WHAT TIME OF DAY IS A GENTLEMAN
MOST LIKELY TO FART?

He is most likely to fart first thing in the morning while
in the bathroom. This is known as 'morning thunder',
and if he gets good resonance it can often be heard
throughout the house. In fact a gentleman's fart is a
more reliable guide to the dawning of a new day than
the traditional cockerel. Indeed, as a gentleman gets
older the cock may not rise first thing in the morning
but the butt will always bellow.

FART FACT #9

A fart is made up of less than
1 per cent of the main chemical
that actually stinks (hydrogen
sulphide), yet its pungency is
such that the human nostril can
detect it at levels of one part
in 100 million.

WHAT IS CROPDUSTING?

Cropdusting is the act of ripping a lethal fart indoors and then moving quickly to the other end of the room in order to stay ahead of your own stench, an action that 'dusts' the room with your flatulence. It is guaranteed to liven up a dull party. It certainly worked well for me at my nephew's christening earlier this year.

WHAT IS THE BEST POSITION FOR FARTING?

This is a question I am often asked, and the simple answer is: any position that allows the gas to escape unhindered. That is why when sitting down it is often advisable to raise one buttock off the seat immediately before a toot. This is known as the five-second warning pose as by adopting this position you warn everyone in the vicinity that a fart is imminent, allowing them the opportunity to flee the premises if they so desire. So if you work with someone who is prone to office flatulence, keep an eye on their buttocks all day. This is based on sound medical advice – at least that's what you can tell the tribunal if you are accused of sexual harassment.

MY WIFE FARTED IN FRONT OF ME.
SHOULD I DIVORCE HER?
Only if it was definitely your turn.

WHEN WORKING AS A WAITRESS AT A TOP HOTEL, I WAS CARRYING IN A TRAY OF AFTERNOON TEA AND SCONES WHEN I SUDDENLY FELT A FIERCE PARP BUILDING UP INSIDE ME. RATHER THAN RISK IT BEING A NOISY ONE IN FRONT OF SUCH DISTINGUISHED GUESTS, I DECIDED TO MASK THE SOUND BY DELIBERATELY DROPPING THE TRAY SO THAT THE FINEST BONE CHINA SHATTERED INTO HUNDREDS OF PIECES. WAS THIS THE RIGHT THING TO DO?

You definitely chose the correct course of action. China is replaceable; dignity is not. I am sure the guests rallied round to help you after the unfortunate 'accident' with the tray. I fear they would have been markedly less sympathetic had you just dropped a snorter in their faces.

IS THERE SUCH A THING AS A FANNY FART?
Although not spoken of in polite society the fanny fart or 'queef' does indeed exist. It is caused by a build-up of air in the lady's vagina, the result of repeated penetration and release during sexual

intercourse. While a queef sounds like an anal fart and possesses the same potential for embarrassment, it is generally odourless and is therefore unlikely to put the gentleman off his stroke once he has stopped laughing. If, however, your girlfriend regularly lets out real stinkers during sex, it may be time to change position . . . or girlfriends.

FART FACT #10

A fart can travel a distance of up to
50 feet depending on wind conditions
or the level of air circulation in a room.
The speed of a fart has been measured
at 10 feet per second, which works out
at about 7mph. However my good wife
has been known to clock more than
twice that speed while fleeing from one
of my most potent cheese cutters.

Modern Farting Etiquette

While it is generally acceptable to fart in the presence of one's friends or immediate family, provided there is adequate ventilation, the question that has taxed the minds of social commentators for centuries is: when is it safe to fart in a relationship? When can you be sure that a gas leak won't spell the end of a promising romance so that when a window opens a door closes? Alec Bromcie in his seminal work

The Complete Book of Farting (Michael O'Mara Books, 1999) advises that all trumps should be held back until the fourth date at the earliest. However, in the intervening years attitudes have changed as women have become ever more liberated and emboldened. Just as some women now choose to drink the same amounts of alcohol as men, they see it as a natural progression to fart the same as men too. But beware, there are many members of the fairer sex – the majority, in fact – who still adhere to old-fashioned principles regarding flatulence, so the trick is to spot into which category your partner falls. For, while a brazen farteuse may merely think you a wimp should you apologize for an untimely toot, firing an eggy arseblast and making a point of sniffing it may not necessarily go down well with a more modest lady. Therefore to avoid disaster when it comes to personal gas it is best to divide women into two types: those who do and those who don't.

Women Who Do

These women have no qualms about letting rip. They can drink their partner under the table and beat him in a farting contest, too. They are happy to sit with him on the sofa all day, watching TV, guzzling beer from the can and helping him make the room smell as if it has just been hired out for a skunk convention. They will not only appreciate his farts, they may even inhale. For many years it was thought that such women were merely figments of warped male fantasies, but they can now be seen by day on *The Jerry Springer Show* and by night rolling around the gutters of most town centres.

Women Who Don't

It must be stressed that for most women flatulence remains one of the last taboos, ranking just below infidelity, bestiality and wearing trainers with a floral dress. However, as we have seen, farting is more than just a hobby: it is a healthy option. We pass wind so many times a day it is inevitable that sooner or later we are going to feel the urge in front of our partner. So when is it deemed acceptable to introduce farting into a relationship? From your first encounter, the matter of personal gas hovers in the background unspoken, unseen and unsniffed. It is akin to finding the right moment to mention a secret love child or erectile dysfunction. It is very much the elephant in the room – and trust me, in some cases it will smell as if there was an elephant in the room.

On a first date it is always best to suppress any wind unless you have decided almost from the outset that this is not the woman for you. In that eventuality as well as getting her to pay for her own drinks, catch the bus home and telling her she could do with losing a few pounds, you can let rip ad nauseam so that she won't be too upset when you tell her you don't want to see her again. You are being cruel to be kind, although in any case she will almost certainly have reached the same conclusion a good twenty minutes before you. Otherwise keep the anal beast secured under lock and key. Don't blow your chances by blowing parps.

As you get to know each other on subsequent meetings, you can start to relax a little, but beware of being too forward. Just as the matter of finding out whether or not she is into bondage and S&M should be tackled delicately, so it is the same with flatulence. You could try working the topic of guffing into the conversation – perhaps by launching a discussion on wind farms – to see how she reacts or you could test the water over dinner by hinting that champagne often makes you a little gassy. If she indicates that she has no problem with that, you can move on to the next level, which involves deliberately letting a quiet one out in a private place, followed, of course, by fulsome apologies. Basically don't try to walk before you can run, although if you have unleashed a wet one you may not be able to do either.

In these modern times the chances are that by the third or fourth date you will probably have slept together. She will have seen that unfortunate birthmark and you will have seen what she looks like first thing in the morning, so a little gas shouldn't prove a relationship wrecker. In any case she will probably have realized by then that excessive flatulence is by no means the worst of your traits. Even so, resist the temptation to boast about your gas – no matter how majestic it is – refrain from gratuitous farting and certainly don't expect her to share your enthusiasm for its scent. Hopefully in time she will be confident enough to release a few toots of her own, but under no circumstances should she be pressured into doing this. She will do so when she is good and ready. Just because she doesn't want to fart with you doesn't mean she has fallen out of love with you – unless, of course, you discover that she has been chuffing away merrily with another man.

Assuming that she does eventually become flatulence-tolerant, it should always remain a private matter between the two of you. Do not invite others to share your fascination in what the tabloids are wont to term 'a three-in-a-bed whump'.

Where Fart Thou, Romeo?
To make sure you know the rules governing gas, try this short quiz based on different scenarios:

1. On your second date, the two of you are enjoying a romantic candlelit dinner in a restaurant when suddenly you feel that telltale build-up in the land beyond your bowels. Should you:

a) Politely excuse yourself from the table and go to the bathroom.
b) Let it rip and hope that the taped flamenco music drowns the sound.

c) Drop your pants and try to blow out the candle with your fart.

Answer a). While an ability to blow out the candle with your butt gas may impress your mates, it is unlikely to be as well received by your girlfriend or indeed by your fellow diners especially if they happen to be sitting downwind of you. In this instance discretion is definitely the better part of valour.

2. You are lying on top of your partner in bed and have just begun making love when your bottom

remembers the family-sized tin of baked beans that you
consumed single-handedly for dinner. Do you say:

a) 'I'm so sorry about that, darling. I hope it
   hasn't put you off.'
b) 'Ooops! It must be the beans I ate for dinner.'
c) 'Jesus wept! That's the seventeenth I've
   dropped today.'
d) 'Oh yes! Yes, yes, yes, yes! What a snorter!
   Don't you just wish you could bottle it?'

Answer a). Consideration for your partner is all-
important in such situations. b) offers too much

information while c) suggests an unhealthy interest
– to the point of obsession – with your gas. And
if your answer is d) you probably need to try a
different diet and relationship counselling.

3. Early in the relationship you are sitting on the
sofa one evening watching TV together when just as
you go to put your arm around her, the movement
causes you to drop one. Should you:

a) Offer to have the sofa re-covered.
b) Blame it on her pet gerbil.
c) Blame it on the squeaky sofa.

d) Say nothing, and hope that it doesn't prove
   to possess the sort of stench that even military
   commanders would hesitate to unleash on
   the enemy.

Answer d). There is no reliable way of predicting whether
or not your fart will be nostril-friendly, so keep quiet –
you may get away with it. On the other hand, lies will
always come back to haunt you, as indeed might your
butt whiff fifteen minutes later when you least expect it.

FART FACT #11

Termites fart more than any other living creature because their diet consists of vegetation and wood. At the other end of the social scale pogonophoran worms, jellyfish and sea anemones don't fart at all because they don't have an anus.

Spot the Farter

THE ATHLETIC FARTER

One who likes to announce the release of each fart by
performing a short gymnastic routine. This usually
involves putting his weight on his left hand and raising his
right buttock off the chair in order to aim the gas blast at
an unfortunate victim. (see also The Yoga Farter)

THE CAREFREE FARTER

One who has absolutely no qualms about letting rip – whether it be in a crowded elevator, a memorial service or on a train in rush hour. He will fart any time, any place, anywhere, for which reason this type of flatulist is also known as the Martini Farter.

THE CONSIDERATE FARTER

One who loves to break wind when his partner is present because he has been told that the secret of a stable relationship is to share things.

THE CUNNING FARTER
One who is able to place a fart in such a way that somebody else will get the blame for it.

THE DISHONEST FARTER
Someone who always denies being responsible for a fart, but will instead blame rotten meat, the dog or climate change. Women make up a large percentage of this category.

THE DUTCH OVEN FARTER
One who farts in bed and then forcibly holds his partner's head under the bedclothes.

THE EXHIBITIONIST FARTER
One who announces to the world, 'Sorry, I've just dropped one' in case nobody has noticed.

THE INEPT FARTER
One who strains to unload a fart but ends up accidentally shitting himself instead.

THE INTELLIGENT FARTER
One who can determine what his neighbour has been eating recently purely from the smell of his fart.

THE MUSICAL FARTER
Not satisfied with polluting the atmosphere, this
artistic farter likes to recreate the intros to popular
tunes using nothing but the sound of his flatulence
(see Farting Tunes).

THE NARCISSISTIC FARTER
One who loves the smell of his own farts.

THE NERVOUS FARTER
One who is so shocked and ashamed by having farted that
he immediately becomes an emotional wreck, to the point

of requiring therapy. If the fart is an SBD,
he may even faint.

THE PHANTOM FARTER
One who is able to drop a discreet stink bomb and
then make himself scarce, leaving others in the
vicinity to look around and wonder whodunit.

THE REFLEX FARTER
One who doesn't guff intentionally, but who does
so in response to a specific incident that has caused
shock or surprise. Such a person's first reaction
to the news that his girlfriend is pregnant will

therefore be to let one go involuntarily. This has been
known to spoil the announcement, particularly if her
parents happen to be present at the time.

THE SAS FARTER
One who sneaks into a crowded room, lets a silent
one go and then sneaks out again. Maximum carnage.
Mission accomplished.

THE SERIAL FARTER
One who just can't stop himself – and doesn't
really want to.

THE THRIFTY FARTER
One who always holds several farts in reserve.

THE UNDERWATER FARTER
One who likes nothing more than to sit in the bathtub and rumble them out like World War II torpedoes heading for the German fleet.

THE UNSOCIABLE FARTER
One who excuses himself and farts in private.

THE YOGA FARTER

One who likes to put on a show by lying on his back and bringing his knees up to his chest so that his butt is in the air. This is not only a good position for being able to appreciate one's gas, it can also help to force out any reluctant toots.

FART FACT #12

In 1665, doctors in London told people to store their farts in a jar and then inhale them to avoid the killer disease known as the Great Plague. It was believed that the plague was caused by deadly vapours in the air, so many doctors thought it could be cured by breathing in an equally foul vapour, such as a fart.

Farting Funnies and Guffing Guffaws

An old woman was riding in an elevator in a Manhattan apartment block when a beautiful young woman stepped in, smelling of expensive perfume. She turned to the old woman and said loftily: 'Romance by Ralph Lauren, $150 an ounce.'

On the next floor another beautiful young woman got into the elevator, also smelling of expensive perfume. She, too, turned to the old woman and sniffed: 'Chanel No. 5, $200 an ounce.'

Three floors later the old woman reached her destination. As she was about to exit the elevator, she looked at the two beautiful young women, bent over, farted and announced: 'Broccoli, 49 cents a pound.'

A woman in a restaurant farted loudly just as the waiter was approaching her table. Knowing that everyone in the place must have heard the noise, she desperately tried to save face by telling the waiter: 'Stop that!'

'Sure, lady,' said the waiter. 'Which way is it headed?'

Two old ladies were comparing the respective merits of stockings and tights.

'I prefer stockings,' said one.

'Me, too,' said the other. 'I think they're more refined and elegant, don't you?'

'Definitely. Besides, if I fart wearing tights I usually blow my slippers off!'

A hobo walked into a Midwest bar and ordered a drink. The bartender said: 'I'll have to see your money first.'

'I'm broke,' admitted the hobo, 'but if you give me two large Scotches I'll get up on that stage and fart "Dixie".'

Thinking that this had to be worth seeing, the bartender agreed. The hobo downed the two large Scotches, staggered on stage and the audience applauded. Then he dropped his pants and the audience cheered wildly. But then he crapped all over the stage and the audience walked out in disgust.

The bartender yelled: 'You said you were gonna fart "Dixie", not crap all over my stage!'

'Hey,' said the hobo. 'Even Frank Sinatra had to clear his throat before he sang!'

What happens when you eat baked beans and peanut butter? You get a fart that sticks to the roof of your ass.

A young man was so nervous about going to his new girlfriend's parents for dinner that he couldn't stop himself passing gas throughout the meal. The first time he did it, the girl's father turned to the family dog which was sitting next to the table and said: 'Rover, get away from the table.' The young man gave an inward sigh of relief and was grateful to the father for getting him out of an embarrassing situation.

Moments later, the young man farted again. Once more, the father turned to the dog and said: 'Rover, move away from the table.'

Shortly afterwards, the hapless young man let another one go. Again the father spared his blushes by telling the dog: 'Rover, move away from the table.'

No sooner had the dog been admonished than
the young man let out a real snorter – louder and
smellier than his previous efforts. The father turned
to the dog and said: 'Rover, for Christ's sake hurry
up and move before he craps all over you!'

A working-class man had been going out with
an upper-class girl for over a month until one
weekend he was invited over for dinner at her
parents' country mansion. Trying his best not to be
intimidated by the sheer size of the house, not to

mention the maids and butlers, he engaged in polite pre-dinner small talk and was relieved when everyone laughed at his jokes. They then sat down for a seven-course meal, which he was determined to get through without embarrassing himself by picking up the wrong item of cutlery.

Everything was going smoothly until about halfway through the meal when the combination of the various rich foods made him want to fart. He desperately tried to hold it in, but with four more courses to go, he realized it would be impossible. So he said he needed to be excused to go to the bathroom and asked for directions as to how to get there. The instructions he received were really complicated, but by then he was busting for a fart, so he decided to set off in search of the bathroom and hope for the best.

After roaming the corridors, hopelessly lost, for a few minutes, he could hold it in no longer. Spotting a window in a hallway, he rushed over, opened the window, stuck his butt through it and let out a long, loud, stinky fart that measured 7.5 on the Richter scale. Hugely relieved, he then managed to find his way back to the dinner table where everyone was eating in silence.

Turning to his girlfriend, he whispered: 'It's all going rather well, isn't it?'

'It was,' she replied frostily, 'until you farted through the serving hatch!'

Alone in an elevator, a smartly dressed rep for a perfume company realized that she could no longer hold in a fart. Immediately after letting it go, she reached into her bag and sprayed the air with deodorizer.

Two floors later, a man got into the elevator
and began to sniff the air.

'Can you smell something?' asked the woman.

'Yes, I can,' said the man.

'What does it smell like?' she persisted.

'Hmmm,' he mused. 'I'd say it smells like
someone crapped in a pine tree.'

An old man and his wife were lying in bed. After a few minutes he let out an almighty fart and shouted: 'Seven points.'

His wife rolled over and asked: 'What in heaven's name was that?'

The old man said: 'Touchdown. I'm ahead seven-nil.'

A few minutes later the wife, entering into the spirit, let one go and declared: 'Touchdown. Tie score.'

But ten minutes later the old man farted again and announced: 'Touchdown. I'm ahead fourteen-seven.'

Not to be outdone, the wife quickly farted again and said: 'Touchdown. Tie score.'

Desperate to regain the lead, the old man strained really hard but he simply couldn't force out a fart. In the end he strained so hard that he pooped in the bed.'

The wife looked at him in disbelief and asked: 'Now what in heaven's name was that?'

The old man replied: 'Half-time. Switch sides.'

What's the difference between a clever spoonerism
and a fart? One's a shaft of wit . . .

A woman went into an exclusive store to buy a rug but as
she bent down to inspect it, she farted loudly. 'I'm terribly
sorry,' she told the salesman. 'It just slipped out.'

The salesman said: 'Lady, if you farted just touching it,
you're gonna crap your pants when you see what
the price is!'

FART FACT #13

In 2008, a farting application
for the iPhone made nearly
$10,000 in one day.

The Future Stinks

If you have ever dropped a really bad one and struck
a match to get rid of the smell, you will notice how
brightly the flame suddenly burns when coming
into contact with the anal emission. You can't
help thinking that therefore the energy harnessed
from your choicest farts could power a small
neighbourhood for several days. Thankfully scientists
have come to similar conclusions and are now

**looking for ways of using bodily gases for the
benefit of humanity.**

Parp parp

Scientists have devised a method of using free
human gas to power small cars. The Fart Car has
been hailed as the Smart Car of the future. Instead
of plugging the vehicle into an outlet or buying gas,
drivers would create their own simply by consuming

copious amounts of baked beans, lentils and Brussels
sprouts before a long journey. They then fart into a tube
that leads into the car's gas tank, where,
to prevent escapes, a valve automatically closes after
each deposit.

Although a prototype car has only travelled a few feet
under human windpower, experts are by no means
downcast and insist that the future for the Fart Car is
looking good, if pungent.

A more practical proposal might be the modified Volkswagen Beetle tested in the UK which runs on compressed methane gas – fart gas – that has been extracted from human waste. The waste from seventy homes can generate enough gas to run the car for 10,000 miles, so the Dung Beetle – as it has been dubbed – could be the answer to rising fuel prices.

Harnessing cows

If you've ever been on the receiving end of a cow's fart you'll know that claims about their methane-rich emissions accounting for 18 per cent of the greenhouse gases that are supposedly warming the planet are not just exaggeration. Luckily, scientists have developed a method for extracting the methane from a cow's backside and converting it into a usable biogas fuel. In Kent County, California, a company called BioEnergy Solutions has harnessed enough fuel from bovine flatulence and poop to power 200,000 homes. Researchers in Argentina – where there are 55 million cattle – have gone even further by creating a bovine backpack that captures a cow's farts via a tube attached to the animal's stomach. The only possible downside is that any blockage or malfunction in the backpack might cause the cow to explode. So beware of a cow wearing a backpack. It could be a terrorist.

Stench seeker

While some scientists are working to find a cure for cancer, others are building devices to measure the quality of your farts. Robert Clain and Miguel Salas, computer engineering students at Cornell University in the US, have designed the Stench Seeker, a machine that grades your farts according to smell, temperature and sound. Featuring a sensitive hydrogen sulphide monitor, a thermometer and microphone, the detector ranks your fart on a scale of 1 to 9. If you force out a 9, a fan helpfully starts up to disperse the stink. The machine will even record the noise so that you can play it back later to anyone you wish to impress.

When presenting their invention in class, Clain and Salas had to test the detector by making raspberry sounds and breathing on it as human exhalations generally contain enough hydrogen sulphide to trigger such a sensor, particularly if you have breath like a smelly sock. 'It's hard to fart something really smelly on command,' lamented Clain. 'Besides, it provided a nicer atmosphere for those around us.' Their professor agreed, and awarded the project a well-deserved A grade.

Classical gas

We have come a long way since the whoopee cushion of yesteryear. Utilizing innovative technology, Man has produced a fart machine that not only replicates fifteen realistic fart sounds, but also operates up to 100 feet away.

The makers of 'Fart Machine No. 2' claim that the device uses 'Boom Box technology' to allow those noxious noises to really reverberate. And what's more, the remote-controlled appliance works through walls, meaning you can really wreak havoc in your home or workplace.

Fart pads

Embarrassed you can't keep it in when in public?
Then why not invest in some fart pads. Laced with
activated charcoal, these ingenious (if not overly
attractive) adhesive pads help neutralize even the
most odiferous of releases.

A lifesaver for anyone suffering from regular
intestinal issues, the pads are worn inside your
underwear and can be used daily or just inserted
when needed. Called Flat-D Flatulence Deodorizers,
they are available online from
<www.colonialmedical.com>.

Blanket effect

Is flatulence ruining your love life? Well, science teacher Francis Bibbo from Denver, Colorado has come up with a solution in the form of the Better Marriage Blanket, a fart-absorbing bedspread that means you'll never again have to blame it on the dog. It is made with stink-absorbing activated carbon fabric – 'the same type of fabric used by the military to protect against chemical weapons'. So even if you start farting mustard gas your partner will be protected. The Better Marriage Blanket is advertised as the ideal anniversary gift, although it's hard to imagine your partner feeling particularly romantic after unwrapping such a package.

The fart silencer

A Chinese designer by the name of Big Chicken
Mushroom has come up with what he calls the
'Ultimate Fart Silencer', a small, torpedo-shaped
device that is filled with a perfumed cotton ball
before being slotted where the sun doesn't shine.
Made of plastic, it is open at one end to catch the
passed gas and has smell holes built into the other
end to prevent the odour and sound making you the
centre of attention whenever you have eaten beans
or cabbage for dinner. Leaving aside the obvious
discomfort of wearing a plastic butt plug, surely
the future of this product will be the opportunity to

create farts in different perfumes and flavours. What girl could resist a man who farts honeysuckle, strawberry or lavender?

Farting doll

The new must-have toy in Korea is a doll that farts. Costing between $22 and $30, Kong Suni serves as a potty training model for children. She eats, she farts when you rub her stomach and she even passes smiley yellow turds. If the idea takes off worldwide, expect to see Farting Barbie soon in a store near you.

Mr Methane

Many observers consider the future of light entertainment to be Mr Methane, an English flatulist following in the footsteps of the celebrated nineteenth-century French farteur Joseph Pujol (aka Le Pétomane). The self-styled 'King of Farts', Cheshire-born Paul Oldfield discovered his unusual talent at the age of fifteen while doing yoga exercises. The next day he performed twenty quickfire rasping farts in under a minute to his friends who were so impressed they asked him to do it on a regular basis on their nights out, which at least ensured they always got a table to themselves in the pub.

After turning professional as Mr Methane, in 1997 he produced a parody of the Phil Collins song 'In the Air Tonight' retitled 'Curry in the Air Tonight'. Citing his 'ability to pass wind in tune and at will', he wrote to the singer for permission to release it, but Collins's manager refused, insisting 'this is a very serious song and we cannot see any reason for it to be taken so lightly'. Labelled 'a true genius' by Howard Stern, Mr Methane achieved a lifelong ambition in 2009 by gatecrashing the auditions for *Britain's Got Talent*, pointing his backside at Simon Cowell and farting out an anal rendition of 'The Blue Danube'. I think Mr Methane spoke for a lot of people in Britain that day.

Tweeting toots

A guy called Randy Sarafan has designed a
futuristic office chair that sends a Twitter message
every time he does a fart. The Fart-O-Matic Twitter
Chair is fitted with a natural gas sensor, a small
computer and a wireless module. Within a matter of
weeks, over 3,000 followers had signed up to receive
Tweets such as 'He farted right on me again' and
'Ugh. That was a gross one'.

Farting clowns

A Dutch clown who specializes in farting can be
hired to ease the tension at funerals. Clown Roelof

van Wijngaarden believes one of the best tactics for making people laugh at funerals is to break wind loudly. He says: 'Imagine adults following the coffin to the burial place. People are using their handkerchiefs, no one dares to speak a word. It's all very solemn. Imagine then this clown whispering to the children and at the same time letting out a fart. The children start to giggle and their parents get a smile on their faces. That's what we do, take the tension away.' He adds on his website: 'I only come when I have been invited by the deceased or by the family. We clearly discuss beforehand why someone wishes to have a clown at their funeral.'

Fart By Mail

A new California-based mail order service called Fart By Mail allows people to send greetings that smell and sound like a real fart. Promising 'farts just like Dad used to make', Fart By Mail uses a non-toxic fart-smelling chemical formula sealed in a clear envelope which comes with a warning that recipients should check the back for more information on what they are holding. But if you really want to surprise someone, you can select the 'Stealth' option where the warning is removed. For Valentine's Day, Fart By Mail offers the 'Forever Fart', an elegant perfume bottle containing 'an odiferous formula for loved ones to cherish fond memories of past flatulence'. They always say that it's a sign of true love when your partner gags.

Fart O Gram

In a similar vein, a company called Fart O Gram has created a service that allows you to send prank farting calls over the phone to show someone you care. You get three free attacks per day but you can also buy credit to spread your air biscuits around. If you're unsure about the recipient's reaction, you can call from an anonymous number. Fart O Gram says the service is as easy as cutting cheese.

Just the job?

They're very big on health matters in China, which probably explains why professional fart smellers can earn $50,000 a year there. Yes, 50K just for sniffing someone's guffs. According to Chinese news sources, the hottest career in health currently revolves around anal analysis. By picking up sweet, savoury, bitter and meaty aromas in personal gas, the professional sniffers are able to identify illnesses and pinpoint their location in the body.

On the rectal stinkometer, highly pungent farts indicate bacterial infection in the patient's bowels or intestines. Meanwhile, a raw fishy or meaty smell could point to an infection in the digestive organs or maybe a tumour in the intestinal lining. And the presence of garlic or chives suggests that the patient is over-indulging in those foods and might consequently be at risk of inflammation of the small or large intestines.

The experts can also ascertain a great deal about a person's health simply by measuring the amount of gas expelled with each fart. An enormous guff suggests that the patient has consumed too much fibre while an insignificant 'pfft' hints at intestinal obstruction.

Those hoping to make a career out of fart sniffing must be aged between eighteen and forty-five, abstain from smoking and alcohol, and be free of any kind of nasal impairment. Safety kit consists of a pair of goggles to guard against cheek flappers that really do make your eyes water. Depending on your point of view, this is either the best or the worst job in the world.

Farting Tunes

We fart so many times a day that it seems a shame to let all that effort and energy go to waste. So the more creative farteurs enjoy the challenge of arranging the timing and pitch of their noisiest butt blasts so that they mimic the introductions to popular songs. The experience gives a whole new meaning to the phrase 'hitting a bum note'. Here are a few tunes you might like to try at home:

'Three Blind Mice'

An ideal one for beginners. Three simple botty
notes are all it takes to recreate the start of the
nursery rhyme. After a portion of Brussels sprouts
you should be able to play this to your children
as a Christmas Day party piece.

'Feelings'

An easily recognizable two-note intro makes
Morris Albert's ballad another suitable tune
for beginners. But remember that the second
note is lower and longer, so you'll need to hold
back sufficient gas for it.

'Spanish Flea'

Recreate the sound of Herb Alpert with some
trumpets of your own. The notes come thick
and fast, so this tune should ideally be performed
after an exceptionally hot curry.

WARNING: an attempt to perform the entire
2 minutes 6 seconds of the piece will almost
certainly result in hospitalization.

'Satisfaction'
Most of us have managed the first two notes of
the Rolling Stones' classic to a standard that
would impress Mick and Keith, but to achieve
the entire intro requires considerable practice
and a lot of lentils. Very much the Holy Grail
for the musical farter.

FART FACT #14

Herring use farting as a means of
communicating with each other.
Scientists found that the creatures
create high-frequency bubbles by
releasing air through their anuses,
enabling fellow herring to get wind
of their presence. Who says that
humans can't learn from fish?